FOSSIL HUNTERS

by Richard Spilsbury

a Capstone company — publishers for children

Engage Literacy is published in the UK by Raintree.
Raintree is an imprint of Capstone Global Library Limited, a company incorporated in England and Wales having its registered office at 264 Banbury Road, Oxford, OX2 7DY – Registered company number: 6695582

www.raintree.co.uk

© 2018 by Raintree. All rights reserved. No part of this publication may be reproduced, stored in a retrieval system, or transmitted in any way or by any means, electronic, mechanical, photocopying, recording or otherwise, without the prior written permission of Capstone Global Library Limited.

Editorial credits
Marissa Kirkman and Jennifer Huston, editors; Richard Parker and Clare Webber, designers; Wanda Winch, media researcher; Kathy LaVigne, production specialist

Image credits
Capstone: Jon Hughes, back cover, 13, 15, 21, 25, 33 (top), 40; Dreamstime: Kiddckho, 41; Getty Images Inc: Field Museum Library/John Weinstein, 38, AFP/GOH CHAI Hin, 37; iStockphoto: Mark Kostich, 14; Library of Congress: Prints and Photographs Division, 24; North Wind Picture Archives, 26; Science Source: James L. Amos, 32; Shutterstock: Avigator Thailand, 11, BarryTuck, 6, berm_teerawat, 20, Bjoern Wylezich, cover (bottom right), chrupka, 33 (b), 34 (t), David Herraez Calzada, cover (bottom left), Edelwipix, 7, Faviel_Raven, 18, 43, jannoon028, 9, Jaroslav Moravcik, 30, Jeff Whyte, 44, JFs Pic Factory, 3, 17, MarcelClemens, 4, Microgen, Cover, Morphart Creation, 16 (top, middle), paleontologist natural, 5, 12, background design, PremiumArt, 31, Ranier Lesniewski, 19, 29, Rattana, 8, Romans_1_20, 34 (b), solarseven, 23, starmaro, 35, vendor, 16 (b), Vlad G, 39, Wlad74, 28, YamabikaY, white paper design; Wikimedia: Ballista, 22

21 20
10 9 8 7 6 5 4 3 2
Printed and bound in India.

Fossil Hunters

ISBN: 978 1 4747 4652 6

CONTENTS

Fantastic fossils 4

How fossils form 6

Finding fossils 10

Early fossil hunters 14

Dinosaur hunters 22

Game changers 28

Big finds 34

New discoveries 42

Timeline 46

Glossary 47

Index 48

FANTASTIC FOSSILS

Have you ever seen or even held a *fossil*? Fossils are the *remains* of plants and animals that lived thousands or even millions of years ago. They are clues to what life was like on Earth in the past.

Fossils mostly formed slowly inside rocks buried underground. This means they are often hidden out of sight. It's up to fossil hunters to find them.

Fossils are clues that many weird and wonderful plants and animals lived on Earth long ago.

Fossil hunters know where the best places on Earth are to search for fossils. They learn all about the living things whose remains turned into fossils. They know how to find and identify fossils and how to get them out of the ground. Over time, some daring fossil hunters have made many amazing discoveries.

FACT: PALAEONTOLOGISTS
Fossil hunters are also known as *palaeontologists*. Palaeontologists are scientists who study the fossils of plants and animals and what they tell us about the history of Earth.

HOW FOSSILS FORM

Fossil hunters know it is best to look for fossils in *sedimentary rocks*. Fossils are often found buried in the layers of this type of rock.

In layers

Sedimentary rocks formed from layers of *sediment* such as mud and sand. Over many years, layers of sediment were buried and pressed down on each other until they became layers of hard rock. Sometimes dead animals or plants became buried under sediment and were trapped in the layers, too.

This cliff was formed over thousands of years as layers and layers of sediment built on top of each other.

Astonishing change

An astonishing change happened to the dead plants and animals in the rock. Water from the rock flowed into the remains, and *minerals* from the water soaked into them. As the minerals dried, they gradually turned into hard stone in the exact shape of the remains.

a *fossilized* leaf that turned into coal

FACT: COAL IS A FOSSIL!
Coal is a black fossil we burn for heat. It formed from the remains of ancient trees that died, fell into swamps and were covered in sediment.

Other types of fossils

Fossils are not just bones and shells. Tracks made in mud or piles of dung (animal waste) can get covered by sediment and become fossils, too. Fossils such as this give clues about an ancient animal's daily life.

Trapped!

Some fossils are animals that got trapped. Some of these animals, such as sabretooth tigers, fell into sticky tar pits where they died. Their bodies sank to the bottom and slowly broke down over time, leaving only their *skeletons* behind.

This fossilized footprint shows how large a dinosaur's foot was compared to a human's.

Ice fossils

Some ancient animals got trapped and buried in cold, soggy soil. They died and were buried in sediment that was frozen. Animals preserved in this deep freeze are only found when the frozen soil thaws out!

FACT: AMBER
In the past, ancient insects, such as tiny flies or spiders, got trapped in sticky tree *resin*. Over time the yellowish brown resin hardened into a substance called *amber*.

FINDING FOSSILS

In the past, people mostly found fossils at the surface of Earth, when rocks crumbled or were worn away. Today fossil hunters can also use tools to find fossils hidden beneath thick layers of hard rock.

Secrets uncovered

Wind, heat, ice, rain and waves can all wear away the surface of rocks. When the upper layers of sedimentary rock wear away, they can uncover buried fossils. Some fossils have been hidden inside layers of rock for thousands of years.

View from above

To find fossils that are still hidden in rocks, today's palaeontologists use pictures taken by *satellites* circling above Earth in space. The pictures show the types of rock and landforms where fossils might be located. Palaeontologists then travel there to hunt for new discoveries.

Palaeontologists discovered this fossilized dinosaur buried for millions of years under layers of rock and sand.

FACT: COMPLETE FOSSILS

Fossil hunters rarely find complete fossilized skeletons. Most of the time, they have to piece together the skeleton from bones scattered all around. They work out what the animal looked like using their knowledge of living animals and other fossils.

Digging up fossils

Once the fossil is found, special drilling tools are used to carefully remove the rock around the fossil. Even with modern tools, digging up fossils is still dusty, tiring work.

Fossil dig

Modern fossil hunters still use some of the same methods used in the past. They use pickaxes or explosives to remove large chunks of rock above a fossil. Then they use tools, such as hammers and chisels, to gently chip away rock closer to the fossil. Finally, they transport the fossil to the lab to study it.

A palaeontologist uses a chisel to chip away the soil and rocks surrounding a dinosaur bone.

Looking inside rocks

Today, palaeontologists also use a machine called a CT scanner to find out exactly where a fossil is located inside a rock. These are the same machines used in hospitals to see inside patients' bodies. Palaeontologists use them to see inside rocks.

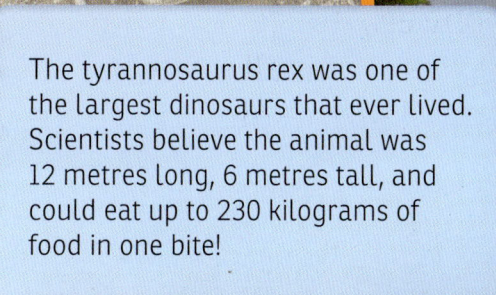

The tyrannosaurus rex was one of the largest dinosaurs that ever lived. Scientists believe the animal was 12 metres long, 6 metres tall, and could eat up to 230 kilograms of food in one bite!

BARNUM BROWN
1873–1963

American palaeontologist Barnum Brown was the first person to find tyrannosaurus rex bones, including the skull. He shielded the dinosaur's bones from damage using plaster casts like those used to protect broken arms and legs. Fossil hunters still use this method today.

EARLY FOSSIL HUNTERS

Hundreds of years ago, people thought fossils were oddly shaped stones, the remains of dragons or even objects that had fallen from the sky.

megalodon tooth

great white shark tooth

FACT: ENORMOUS SHARK!
The largest fossilized shark teeth ever found were 18 centimetres long. Great white shark teeth are only a third as long. Because the teeth were so large, scientists believe they came from a huge fish such as the giant shark megalodon. Megalodon fossils show that it was three times larger than the great white shark, with a mouth wide enough to swallow a hippo!

Steno's teeth

In 1666 a doctor called Nicholas Steno was examining a big shark caught by fishermen when he realized its teeth looked just like tongue stones. Tongue stones were triangular stones that people at the time thought grew inside rocks. Steno realized that the tongue stones were fossilized shark teeth from the mouths of ancient sharks.

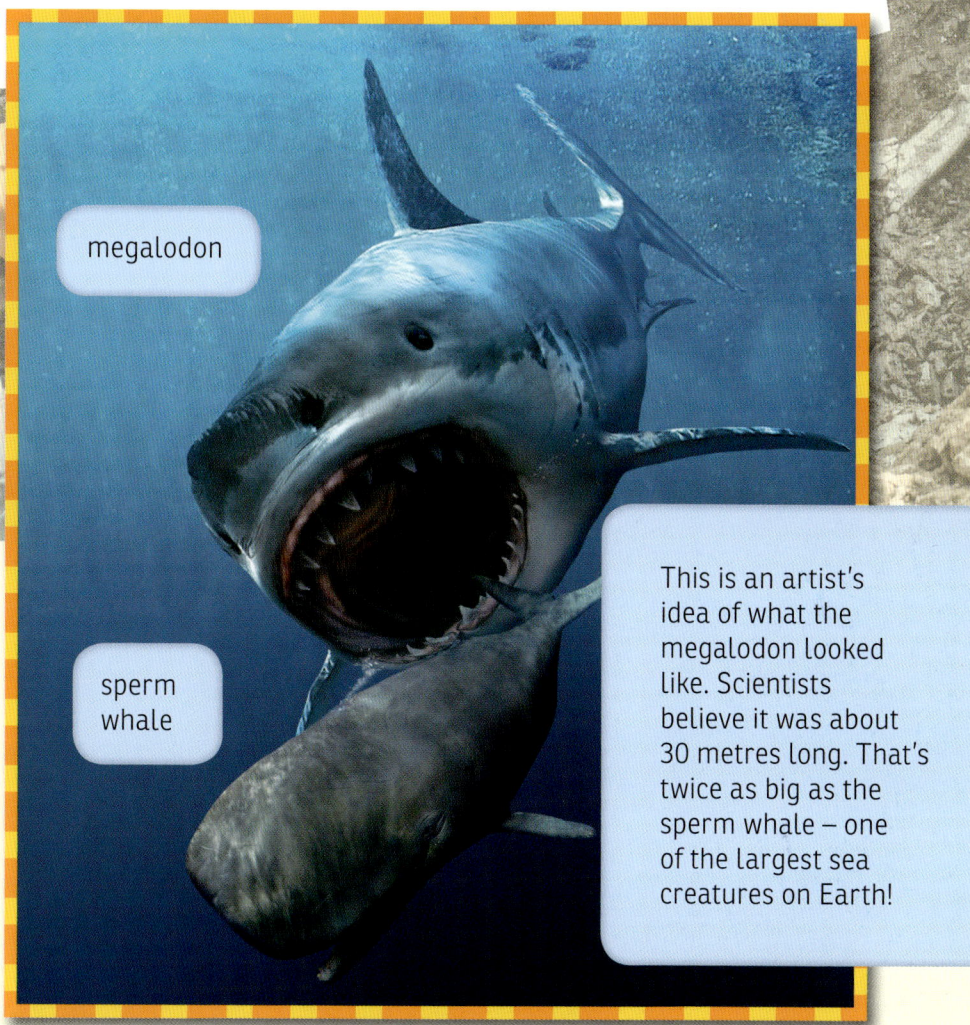

This is an artist's idea of what the megalodon looked like. Scientists believe it was about 30 metres long. That's twice as big as the sperm whale – one of the largest sea creatures on Earth!

In the layers

After his discovery of fossilized shark teeth, Steno studied rock layers in cliffs and hills near where he lived. He studied how tongue stones and other fossils got into the layers.

Youngest on top

Steno came up with the idea that layers of rock formed at the bottom of oceans, trapping the remains of living things inside them. That meant that younger layers of rock formed on top of older ones, so the deeper fossils were found, the older they were.

Extinct

Later scientists realized that some fossils were unlike anything alive on Earth. This told them that the fossils must have been from animals that had died out or had become *extinct*. They worked out when these animals became extinct by finding the last rock layer that had those types of fossils in it.

By studying the rock layers, fossil hunters discovered that ammonites, such as the one shown here, lived around 65 million to 200 million years ago.

FACT: SNAKESTONES?
Ammonites were once called snakestones because they look like coiled snakes. They were really squids with curly shells. They lived in shallow seas and swam by squirting water from their shells.

MARY ANNING

1799–1847

Mary Anning lived in Lyme Regis, England. She started hunting for fossils when she was a child. She rushed out to nearby beaches after storms that made cliffs crumble away. She sold the fossils she found to make money for her family.

When Anning was about 12 years old, she and her brother found the first complete ichthyosaur skeleton. These large ocean *reptiles* with long jaws died out more than 90 million years ago.

a plaster cast of an ichthyosaur skeleton

England's Jurassic Coast

— Jurassic Coast

Lyme Regis is located on the Jurassic Coast of southern England. Fossils dating back 185 million years have been found along this stretch of coastline.

FACT: AMAZING ICHTHYOSAURS
Ichthyosaurs were a bit like dolphins. They swam in the sea catching fish and squid in their long jaws.

Anning's discoveries

Anning went on to make many more amazing discoveries. She found fossilized dinosaur dung as well as fossils from sharks, fish and other ancient creatures.

Finding fame

In 1823 she made her biggest discovery on the Lyme Regis beaches – a complete plesiosaur skeleton. When a famous palaeontologist called Georges Cuvier saw her drawing of the plesiosaur, he thought it was a fake. When he realized his mistake, he helped to make Anning's find famous around the world.

The complete plesiosaur skeleton that Anning found is now in the National History Museum in London.

Based on the complete plesiosaur skeleton found by Anning, scientists believe this is what the creatures looked like.

Flying reptiles

Anning used a pointed hammer to tap pebbles and stones open to uncover fossils. On a dig in Lyme Regis in 1828, she found a complete pterodactylus. This small flying reptile also lived during the time of the dinosaurs.

Recognizing Anning's importance

Although many of Anning's findings ended up in museums, her name was not listed as having discovered them. Many scientists at the time were men. Many of those men did not believe that a woman, such as Anning, who had little schooling, could know as much about fossils as they did. Anning couldn't join the British Geological Society because women weren't allowed to join at the time. But this group of scientists did record her death in 1847. Such an act during this time in history proved that the group realized how important Anning had been. The first woman was allowed to join the British Geological Society in 1904.

DINOSAUR HUNTERS

In 1842 palaeontologist Richard Owen named a new group of fossilized animals. He called them dinosaurs, which means "terrible lizards".

Diverse dinosaurs

By then many different types of dinosaur bones had been found. Dinosaurs came in many shapes and sizes. It was clear from the number of fossils that dinosaurs had once ruled Earth. Many palaeontologists became expert dinosaur hunters who raced to find and name new types of dinosaurs.

Richard Owen

FACT: THE END OF DINOSAURS

No dinosaur fossils younger than 65 million years old have ever been found. Scientists believe this is because all dinosaurs died around the same time. One idea is that a giant *meteorite* hit Earth. Another is that lots of volcanoes erupted, spilling hot lava across the land. The dust thrown up by these events may have filled the air and blocked the amount of sunlight reaching the planet. This could have changed the planet's climate so much that dinosaurs could not survive.

OTHNIEL CHARLES MARSH

1831–1899

Othniel Charles Marsh

As soon as he could explore outdoors, young Othniel Charles Marsh was fascinated by nature. His interest in fossils began after a friend showed him where to find some near his home.

The making of a museum

In 1866 Marsh convinced his uncle to donate money to help Yale University in Connecticut, USA, create the Peabody Museum of Natural History. That year, Marsh also became professor of palaeontology at Yale, the first job of its type in the United States.

Naming finds

Marsh worked at the university until he died. During that time he wrote 300 papers and books about fossils. He also discovered and named about 500 extinct animals, such as toothed birds, huge horned *mammals* and early horses. He also named many dinosaurs including apatosaurus, stegosaurus and triceratops.

24

FACT: ARMCHAIR SCIENTIST?

Marsh is sometimes accused of being an "armchair scientist" because after his first four fossil hunting trips, he stayed at home and let teams of students do the hunting.

Marsh gave the triceratops its name. It means "three-horned face".

Bone Wars!

Marsh's main rival was dinosaur hunter Edward Cope. Marsh and Cope started out as friends, but they soon became enemies as they struggled to see who could find more new dinosaurs.

Beginnings

The so-called "Bone Wars" began when Marsh paid Cope's assistants to send fossil finds to him, instead of Cope. Then in 1870, Cope put a skull on the wrong end of a fossilized skeleton, and Marsh made a fool of him over this mistake.

Edward Cope

Spies!

Marsh and Cope each had teams of people helping them to find fossils. Both Marsh and Cope made their teams spy on each other. The teams also stole each other's fossils and even blew up each other's dig sites. Back in their labs, Cope and Marsh raced against each other to discover and name new fossils.

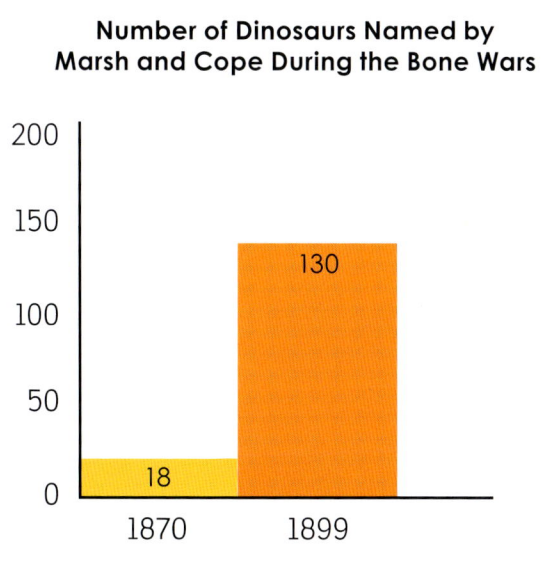

Number of Dinosaurs Named by Marsh and Cope During the Bone Wars

FACT: WHO WON?
The Bone Wars ended in the late 1890s when both men died. In total, the two fossil hunters named more than 130 new dinosaurs. But they lost their fortunes and many friends along the way.

GAME CHANGERS

Some fossil hunters made discoveries that completely changed peoples' ideas of Earth's history. In 1909 Charles Walcott found fossils from 500 million years ago. Before this no one had any idea so many different animals had been alive then.

This famous archaeopteryx fossil is probably the most ancient bird yet discovered.

FACT: ARCHAEOPTERYX

In 1861 a *quarry* worker in Germany found the first fossilized feather. Then palaeontologist Hermann von Meyer found a complete fossilized animal with a skeleton a bit like a dinosaur's but also with feathers. He called it archaeopteryx.

Walcott's finds at Burgess Shale are special partly because it is rare to find fossils of soft-bodied animals.

Walcott's worms

Walcott read reports of strange "stone bug" fossils found by railway workers in the Canadian Rocky Mountains. The stone bugs turned out to be the remains of unknown animals such as worms with legs and unusual shrimp. Over the next 14 years, Walcott spent each summer digging at the Burgess Shale site with his family. In total they found 65,000 fossils.

Dinosaur eggs

Today most of us know dinosaurs hatched from eggs. But less than 100 years ago, people thought dinosaurs gave birth to live young because no one had found any whole fossilized eggs.

A cracking find!

Things changed in 1923 when American palaeontologist Roy Chapman Andrews led a fossil hunt to the Gobi Desert in Mongolia. There, his assistant George Olsen found three fossilized eggs near a stone ledge. Olsen cleared sand away to find a skeleton and 13 more eggs. Andrews and the team started digging in the area and found other dinosaur nests. The fossilized eggs soon became famous worldwide.

dinosaur eggs

ROY CHAPMAN ANDREWS
1884–1960

American palaeontologist Roy Chapman Andrews travelled as far away as Asia on his fossil hunting trips. He wrote popular books about his travels, which included stories about being chased by wild dogs and falling off cliffs.

JACK HORNER

1946–present

Jack Horner was born with a talent for fossil hunting. He found his first dinosaur bone when he was just 8 years old.

First fossil job

As an adult, Horner worked as a truck driver and hunted for fossils at the weekend. After writing to many museums, he got a job at Princeton University's Natural History Museum in New Jersey, USA. There, he began using his skills to discover new dinosaurs and learn about the way they lived.

Dinosaur parenting

In Montana, USA, in 1978, Horner discovered a new type of dinosaur, which he named the maiasaura. This large dinosaur had fossils of its young in its nest. This fossil find showed that maiasauras cared for their young, which lived in the nest after hatching from eggs.

Maiasauras lived and cared for their babies in the nest around 74 million years ago.

FACT: EGG MOUNTAIN!

Horner and his team also found groups of dinosaur nests. This showed that some dinosaurs lived in groups or herds. The hillside in Montana, USA, where he made these discoveries is now called Egg Mountain.

Montana

UNITED STATES

BIG FINDS

California

Every fossil hunter dreams of making a big discovery. But what about thousands of fossils in a pit near a major US city?

Around 3 million fossils have been found in the La Brea tar pits in Los Angeles, California, USA.

FACT: OIL TO TAR
Oil comes from the remains of tiny fossilized sea creatures. Over time, they were heated and pressed inside layers of heavy rocks until they formed a liquid, called oil. Sometimes oil seeps into surface soil. Some oil *evaporates* leaving very sticky tar pits.

Stuck in tar

People often found bones in the tar pits at La Brea Ranch, in Los Angeles, California, USA. They came to the pits to get tar, which is used to prevent water leaks on roofs and on boats. Most people thought the bones were from cattle, but in 1875 people started to realize that the bones might be dinosaur fossils.

Pit digs

In 1912 fossil hunter John C Merriam and his team started a major dig at the La Brea tar pits. They discovered thousands of fossils that had gotten stuck in the tar 8,000 to 40,000 years ago. These included sabretooth tigers, wolves, giant ground sloths, camels and even giant birds.

a sabretooth tiger skeleton

Dinosaur graveyard

In 1979 palaeontologist Dong Zhiming spotted builders in south-west China blasting a hillside to make a car park. Zhiming went over to look and saw the builders had uncovered a dinosaur graveyard.

Bulldozers!

The builders were crushing the bones flat with bulldozers to level the ground. Zhiming got permission to stop the construction and for his team to start digging. In the following years, they found more than 100 different types of dinosaur skeletons as well as fossilized turtles, fish and other animals.

The dinosaur fossils Zhiming found were 170 million years old. They were the first dinosaur bones from that time period discovered in China.

Zhiming's preserved dig site is now the home of the Zigong Dinosaur Museum.

DONG ZHIMING

1937–present

Dong Zhiming decided to become a palaeontologist after seeing a dinosaur *exhibition* in China when he was 13 years old. He went on to become one of the world's busiest palaeontologists using his skill at finding dinosaur fossils.

Perfect skeleton

Most dinosaur skeletons that have been discovered are not complete. They need to be put back together with only some of the animal's bones, many of which are damaged. The most complete skeleton of one of the largest dinosaurs, tyrannosaurus rex, was found by chance in 1990.

A tyrannosaurus rex called Sue

Palaeontologist Sue Hendrickson was walking her dog while on a dig in South Dakota, USA, when she spotted three fossil bones sticking out of a cliff. Hendrickson and her team soon started digging. After three weeks they had removed 9 metres of rock and dug out the parts of a whole tyrannosaurus rex skeleton.

The team called the skeleton Sue. It is the most complete tyrannosaurus rex skeleton ever found, and its bones are well preserved. Palaeontologists have learned more about the tyrannosaurus rex by studying Sue.

The Field Museum in Chicago, Illinois, USA, is home to Sue, the most complete tyrannosaurus rex skeleton ever found.

FACT: PATIENT WORK

Sue is made up of 250 bones and teeth. It took museum staff more than 30,000 hours to remove rock from these parts, clean them, and make them into a complete skeleton.

Mammoth finds!

During a warm spell in Siberia in 2007, Yuri Khudi spotted what he thought was a dead reindeer calf lying on the ground in the distance. Up close, Khudi realized his mistake – this animal had a trunk.

FACT: HAIRY ELEPHANTS
Woolly mammoths such as the one from Siberia are extinct cousins of elephants. They were covered with thick, shaggy hair to keep them warm because they lived hundreds of thousands of years ago during an *ice age*, when much of Earth was covered in ice.

Defrosted fossils

Khudi had found a baby woolly mammoth, which had died about 40,000 years ago. It had been preserved in frozen soil until it thawed. The soil around the animal had then washed away. Other woolly mammoths had been found before, but none like this. This one had hair on its skin and even remains of its last meal, which was milk, in its stomach. Khudi called the baby woolly mammoth Lyuba, after his wife.

Palaeontologists used chemicals to preserve Lyuba's skin. Now its skin looks a bit like crumpled paper.

NEW DISCOVERIES

In 2005 a new type of dinosaur was found when Bill Shipp of Montana, USA, stumbled across its bones. The dinosaur was nicknamed Judith because the bones were found near the Judith River. Judith had horns on her face like the triceratops, except they went sideways rather than sticking straight out.

In 2014 a team of palaeontologists came across large fossilized skulls sticking out of the desert in Tunisia, North Africa. By chance they had discovered the largest crocodile fossil ever found. It was around 10 metres long, which is about twice the length of modern crocodiles.

Completing the puzzle

Each year fossil hunters make amazing new discoveries all over the world. Each new fossil discovery is important. That's because it fills a gap in our knowledge of Earth's history, much like adding pieces to a jigsaw puzzle to complete the final picture.

FACT: CHANGING WORLD

Finding the remains of ancient crocodiles in deserts and fossilized trees in Antarctica are two examples of how fossils show us that the world has changed. They prove that oceans once covered different areas of the planet and that cold places were once much hotter.

Several casts of Judith's skull were made. This one is on display in a museum in Austria.

How to become a fossil hunter

Anyone can find fossils. You just need to know where to look and what to look for. The first thing to do is read all you can about fossils and learn how to identify sedimentary rock by its layers.

The Royal Tyrrell Museum in Canada (pictured here) is home to more than 110,000 fossils.

Where to look

Just like fossil hunters in the past, the best places to look for fossils are old quarries or beaches near cliffs of sedimentary rock. To stay safe, it is best to find a planned tour to hunt for fossils.

Fossil-hunting gear

Fossil hunters wear hard hats to protect them from falling rocks. Safety goggles shield their eyes from tiny pieces of rocks and dust that can fly out when splitting open stones to find fossils inside.

FACT: MEET A FOSSIL

Would you like to see some fossils up close? You can visit a museum to see some great fossils up close and learn about fossil discoveries. You can also go to the museum's website to learn more. Here are some museums with large collections of fossils:

Fernbank Museum of Natural History, Atlanta, Georgia, USA

Field Museum of Natural History, Chicago, Illinois, USA

National Dinosaur Museum, Canberra, Australia

Natural History Museum, London, England

Royal Tyrrell Museum, Drumheller, Alberta, Canada

The Wyoming Dinosaur Center & Dig Sites, Thermopolis, Wyoming, USA

Timeline

1666 Nicholas Steno identifies fossilized shark teeth in Italy.

1811 In Lyme Regis, England, Mary Anning discovers the first complete ichythosaur skeleton.

1823 Mary Anning finds the first complete plesiosaur skeleton.

1861 Hermann von Meyer discovers and describes the first archaeopteryx in a quarry in Germany.

1870–1899 Othniel Charles Marsh and Edward Cope compete in the "Bone Wars" to see who can find and name the most dinosaur fossils.

1901 Palaeontologists start to dig up sabretooth tigers, wolves, giant ground sloths, giant birds and other fossilized animals in the La Brea tar pits in California, USA.

1902 In Montana, USA, American palaeontologist Barnum Brown discovers tyrannosaurus rex bones for the first time.

1909 At the Burgess Shale site in British Columbia, Canada, Charles Walcott finds a huge group of fossils of soft-bodied creatures.

1923 Roy Chapman Andrews finds the first fossilized dinosaur eggs in the Gobi Desert in Mongolia.

1978 Jack Horner discovers fossils of a maiasaura dinosaur and its nest of young in Montana, USA.

1979 Dong Zhiming discovers a dinosaur graveyard in south-west, China.

1990 In South Dakota, USA, Sue Hendrickson discovers the most complete tyrannosaurus rex skeleton ever found.

2005 Bill Shipp discovers a previously unknown type of dinosaur that scientists nickname Judith.

2007 Yuri Khudi discovers a perfectly preserved baby woolly mammoth in Siberia.

2014 In the Sahara Desert in Tunisia, North Africa, palaeontologists discover the largest crocodile fossil ever found.

Glossary

amber yellowish brown substance made from fossilized tree resin

evaporate change from a liquid into a gas

exhibition public display of objects such as fossils or paintings in a museum or gallery

extinct no longer living; an extinct species is one that has died out, with no more of its kind

fossil remains or traces of plants and animals that are preserved as rock

fossilize become a fossil over time

ice age period of time when Earth was covered in ice; the last ice age ended about 11,500 years ago

mammal warm–blooded animal that breathes air; mammals have hair or fur; female mammals feed milk to their young

meteorite chunk of rock that hits a planet; when it travels through space before it lands, it is called a meteoroid

mineral material found in nature that is not an animal or plant

palaeontologist scientist who studies fossils

quarry place where stone is dug out of the ground

remains parts of something that was once alive

reptile cold-blooded animal that breathes air and has a backbone; most reptiles lay eggs and have scaly skin

resin sticky substance that comes from the sap of some trees

satellite spacecraft that circles Earth to gather and send back information

sediment mixture of tiny bits of rock, shells, plants, sand and minerals

sedimentary rock rock formed by layers of rocks, sand or clay that have been pressed together over time

skeleton bones that support and protect the body of a human or other animal

Index

amber 9
ammonites 17
Bone Wars 26–27, 46
British Geological Society 21
Burgess Shale 29, 46
Canadian Rocky Mountains 29
coal 7
dinosaur eggs 30
dinosaurs 13, 20, 21, 22, 24, 26, 27, 28, 30, 32, 33, 35, 36, 37, 38, 39, 42, 45, 46
    apatosaurus 24
    archaeopteryx 28, 46
    ichthyosaur 18, 19, 46
    maiasaura 32, 33, 46
    megalodon 14, 15
    plesiosaur 20
    pterodactylus 21
    stegosaurus 24
    triceratops 24, 25, 42
    tyrannosaurus rex 13, 38–39, 46
Egg Mountain, Montana, USA 33
Gobi Desert 30, 46
ice age 40
Judith (dinosaur) 42, 46
Jurassic Coast 19
La Brea tar pits 34–35, 46
Lyme Regis, England 18, 19, 20, 21, 46
Lyuba (baby woolly mammoth) 41
minerals 7
museums
    Fernbank Museum of Natural History (Atlanta, Georgia, USA) 45
    Field Museum of Natural History (Chicago, Illinois, USA) 39, 45
    National Dinosaur Museum (Canberra, Australia) 45
    Natural History Museum (London, England) 20, 45
    Natural History Museum (Princeton, New Jersey, USA) 32
    Peabody Museum of Natural History (New Haven, Connecticut, USA) 24

(*museums continued*)
    Royal Tyrrell Museum (Drumheller, Alberta, Canada) 45
    Wyoming Dinosaur Center & Dig Sites (Thermopolis, Wyoming, USA) 45
    Zigong Dinosaur Museum (Zigong, China) 37
oil 34
palaeontologists
    Andrews, Roy Chapman 30, 31, 46
    Anning, Mary 18, 20–21, 46
    Brown, Barnum 13, 46
    Cope, Edward 26–27, 46
    Cuvier, Georges 20
    Hendrickson, Sue 38, 46
    Horner, Jack 32, 33, 46
    Khudi, Yuri 40–41, 46
    Marsh, Othniel Charles 24–27, 46
    Merriam, John C 35
    Olsen, George 30
    Owen, Richard 22
    Steno, Nicholas 15–16, 46
    von Meyer, Hermann 28, 46
    Walcott, Charles 28–29, 46
    Zhiming, Dong 36, 37, 46
Princeton University 32
resin 9
sabretooth tigers 8, 35, 46
satellites 10
sedimentary rock 6, 10, 44, 45
Shipp, Bill 42, 46
snakestones, 17
Sue (tyrannosaurus rex) 38–39
tar pits 8, 34–35, 46
tools 10, 12
    chisels 12
    CT scanner 13
    explosives 12
    hammers 12, 21
    pickaxes 12
woolly mammoths 40–41, 46
Yale University 24